Compete on Awesome, not on Price

2024

Susan Frew

From Susan: I dedicate this book to my husband, William Frew, for always believing in me before I believed in myself.

To my fellow warriors navigating the complex paths of head injuries and ADHD,

This dedication is for you – the tenacious souls who transform what others may see as hurdles into unique superpowers. Each day, you navigate a world that isn't always designed for how your mind works or for the aftermath of injuries that have altered your life's trajectory.

I see you, and I commend you. Like you, I've faced the challenges of ADHD and the profound impact of head injuries. These experiences, while daunting, have become integral to my strength and success. They've honed my focus, sparked my creativity, and equipped me with rare and invaluable resilience.

Our journeys are unique, yet they share a thread of relentless determination and an unyielding spirit. Embrace your distinct perspective and your unparalleled resilience. Remember, what some might see as limitations, we can wield as our greatest strengths.

Your journey, like mine, is one of triumph, not despite your ADHD and head injuries but because of them. Your experiences are not just challenges; they are the forge in which your character and abilities are made more robust and distinct.

Keep harnessing your superpowers. The world needs the unique light you shine, the unorthodox solutions you bring, and the inspiring resilience you embody. With admiration and solidarity, Susan Frew

Acknowledgments

There is a kinship among entrepreneurs, a bond forged in the fires of ambition and perseverance. This book aims to strengthen that bond, to offer a hand in the darkest hours, and to celebrate the triumphs that often go unnoticed. My story, intertwined with the stories of many, is a reminder that every step, no matter how heavy, is a stride toward our aspirations. Yet, it is also a reminder that the journey is enriched by the people who walk alongside us.

Let this book be a gentle nudge to keep going to those who find themselves at a crossroads, to the weary souls contemplating giving up. Put one foot in front of the other, for the path of entrepreneurship is walked one step at a time. May these pages be your companion, whispering courage when the shadows loom and rejoicing with you in the light of new dawns.

Your journey is unique, yet it resonates with countless others who share your dreams and fears. In sharing my story, I hope to illuminate yours and bring comfort in the road less traveled. Remember, it is the people, not the business metrics, that truly define our success and fulfillment.

Contents

Introduction

In the business world, the path to success isn't just about hard work; it's about intelligent strategy. I'm living proof of this truth. Blessed with a life filled with love and resilience, I've journeyed from being a former International General Manager at AT&T Wireless and a Business Coach to shaping a business that soared from $177,000 in annual revenue to over $3 million in just 18 months. My life, interwoven with both personal triumphs and adversity—including ten concussions and 16 broken bones from various life events—has been a testament to the power of perseverance and strategic thinking.

However, life took an unexpected turn when my husband became seriously ill. This challenge prompted us to scale down our business to fit our new lifestyle. Despite this shift, I have embraced the opportunity to do what I love: keynote speaking, podcasting, and playing with AI all day. In fact, for our 2024 budget, we were able to save $170,000 by leveraging AI. My mission now is to share this message with others, offering a story of hope about the vast opportunities AI presents. If I can do it, so can you!

This book is more than a story of my family business's exponential growth. It's about the strategic genius behind finding and dominating an underserved market, placing the right people in pivotal roles, and embracing technology as if your survival depended on it. My journey with my husband, William, a master plumber, and an expert in heating and solar thermal technology, is a narrative of harnessing these three key elements to transform our business.

We ventured into a fiercely competitive market with over 950 contenders, where competing on price was not an option. Instead, Automate the ordinary and Personalize the extra ordinary—a concept inspired by the small yet mighty pufferfish, known for its ability to appear larger and more formidable than it is. This metaphor perfectly encapsulates our approach: finding strength in apparent vulnerability, turning our small size into our most significant advantage.

Our strategy was threefold: We identified a niche in the saturated market of Denver. We recognized the need for exceptional customer service in an industry often overlooked for such. We then aligned our business with the right people, ensuring that each team member was competent and in the proper role to contribute effectively. And crucially, we embraced technology wholeheartedly, understanding its power to revolutionize how we operated and connected with our customers.

In this book, I will take you through the highs and lows of our journey, showing how these three strategies can be applied across any industry. I will share the lessons we learned, the successes we celebrated, and the failures that taught us invaluable lessons. This is not just a manual for business growth; it's a beacon of hope for entrepreneurs who feel overwhelmed by their challenges. It's a call to rethink your approach, to find joy in marketing, to embrace innovation, and ultimately, to transform your business into a force to be reckoned with—much like the pufferfish in the vast ocean of competition.

Let this story inspire you to do things differently, to find your unique path in the business world, and to become not just successful but truly remarkable in your endeavors.

CHAPTER 1

HTSA Edition

"Compete on Awesome Not on Price"

Forward by Keith Esterly and Tom Doherty, HTSA

August 2024

As members of the Home Technology Specialists of America (HTSA), we have always prided ourselves on being ahead of the curve—both in the technology we deploy, the processes we adopt, and the experiences we create for our clients. Our mantra, *"Ahead of the Curve,"* isn't just a catchy slogan; it's the foundation of our approach to business. When I first encountered Susan's *"Compete on Awesome Not on Price,"* it struck me how closely aligned her principles are with the values and practices we've cultivated at HTSA. This book is more than just a guide; it's a mirror reflecting our successes, a validation of our efforts, and a challenge to continue pushing the boundaries of excellence. So, I ask: *"Are you in?"* Read on and decide.

HTSA and the Philosophy of Competing on Awesome

In every chapter of this book, you'll find echoes of the strategies we already embrace at HTSA. Susan emphasizes that the path to lasting success is not paved by being the cheapest option, but by being the best option. This is a philosophy that resonates deeply with our own. Our *Relationship Science* program is a testament to this, leading the industry not just in our approach to selling skills but, more importantly, in the relentless commitment to delivering unforgettable, unparalleled client experiences. We aim to exceed our clients' expectations by delivering 116%, exceeding their expectations and far surpassing any mere 100% mark they might anticipate. We aim for the long-term relationship, not the mere transaction. Our one goal is to become their expert friend in the business, for life. And that profoundly changes the way we treat them, the way we handle obstacles, the way we operate as a group. It's about delivering more than just a product—it's about delivering joy, satisfaction, and a sense of security that their investment in us is the right choice. Awesome. Not price.

The Power of Positivity: Green-Brain Theory

One of the key elements that distinguishes HTSA from others in our field is our *Green-brain theory*. Red-brain/Green-brain has gone viral across the group. In her book, Susan speaks to the importance of creating the same type of environment, one which fosters (even *insists* on) positivity, collaboration, and joy—a concept that we at HTSA have taken to heart. A savvy reader will also recognize a ton of "Cialdini" within these pages, examples of ethical influence put into practice to generate good will (a.k.a. Green-brain) in the minds of our clients.

By operating in a "green" state, we not only hire right and keep our teams energized and motivated but also extend that energy to our clients. When our team members approach each interaction with a positive mindset, it transforms the client experience. They feel the difference, and it solidifies our reputation as the best, not just in terms of technology, but in the human connection we cultivate. We deliver Awesome.

Reaching for New Vines

While effective and exciting, Susan's approach doesn't pretend to be easy. But that will not hinder us. Our members are all about letting go of the old vine and reaching for the new one before the old momentum ebbs. This isn't just what we do at

HTSA, it's who we are. In our rapidly evolving industry, clinging to old processes, technologies, or even mindsets can be a recipe for obsolescence. We encourage our members to always be on the lookout for new vines—whether that's the latest in smart home technology, cutting-edge installation processes, or innovative ways to improve your business and enhance the client experience. This willingness to embrace the new is what keeps us at the forefront of the industry. It's what keeps us Awesome.

Our mission isn't just to follow trends; it's to set them. That means continually challenging ourselves to adopt the newest technologies and processes, not just for the sake of being modern, but to enhance the value we provide to our clients.

Who introduced the industry to the Lighting category, and continues to be the unquestioned leader in the category? HTSA. Who is at the cutting edge of AI education and implementation? We are. Heck, Tom and I deliberately used AI to create the early drafts of this foreword in my voice and talking about our core concepts, and after only an hour of refining created this (hopefully) concise, impactful, fully human and fully HTSA tract. We don't just talk about it, we live it. That's Awesome.

Ahead of the Curve: Always Innovating

Staying ahead of the curve requires more than just keeping up; it requires leading. This book reinforces this, urging us not to rest on our laurels but to continue innovating. At HTSA, we don't compete on price because we know that our value lies in the unparalleled quality and service we provide. It's this relentless pursuit of awesome that has built our reputation and will continue to set us apart in the future.

As you dive into this book, consider what your next new vine will be. Is it a new technology that will revolutionize the way your clients live? A new approach to service that will set a new standard for excellence? Or perhaps a new mindset that will inspire your team to reach new heights?

I urge you to read with an eye for both recognition and discovery. You'll see many of the principles we already advocate reflected in its pages—principles that have driven your success and that of HTSA as a whole. But don't stop there. Look for the new vines, the new ideas, and the new approaches that can take you and your business to the next level.

A Call to Action

In closing, I urge you to not just read this book, but to ponder its lessons, be inspired by its insights, and, most importantly, take action. Our mission is to stay ahead of the curve, and that requires not just knowing what to do, but doing it. Let this book be both a celebration of what you've achieved and a roadmap to what comes next. I'll ask again: *"Are you in?"* I hope so.

Stay you. Stay awesome. Stay *Ahead of the Curve*.

Keith Esterly & Tom Doherty, HTSA, August 2024

CHAPTER 2

How to Compete on Awesome With AI

In a world where businesses often default to price wars, breaking the mold is crucial. Competing on excellence, not price isn't just a strategy; it's a mindset that champions quality, innovation, and uniqueness. This chapter is dedicated to sharing my journey and insights on how you can transform your business approach.

Embrace Excellence as Your Business Mantra

Gone are the days when being the cheapest was enough to win the market. Today, it's about offering something extraordinary. Let's take the story of Frontier Airlines as an inspiration. Their decision to feature more significant, more prominent animal images on their planes wasn't just about aesthetics; it symbolized their commitment to connecting with their customers on a deeper level. The inclusion of Marty the Marmot, a result of persistent requests from school children, wasn't just a marketing stunt; it was a testament to their commitment to community involvement and creating memorable experiences.

What can you do in your business to make memorable experiences for your clients? Let this book be the SPARK you need to go out *there and CRUSH your competition.*

The Pillars of Competing on Awesome

To build a business that competes on excellence, focus on these critical areas:

1. Excellence in Service and Products:

Always strive for the highest quality in everything you offer. Your products and services should meet and exceed expectations. Always go for the TECHNOLOGY option first; NEXT, find the manual option.

2. Stellar Networking:

Networking transcends the mere act of exchanging business cards at events; it is the art of cultivating significant connections that can pivot the trajectory of both your professional and personal spheres. It's about engaging in conversations that go beyond the superficial, planting seeds for collaborations that yield a robust harvest of opportunities and shared success. Through my dedicated efforts in networking and speaking engagements, I have forged a web of relationships that has tangibly benefited my business, with my network alone ushering in revenues exceeding $500,000 annually. This figure is a testament not just to the potential of networking but to the profound impact that investing in genuine relationships can have on one's business. It's a strategic approach where every handshake has the potential to open new doors, and every interaction is a step towards mutual advancement.

3. Exceptional Customer Experience:

Elevating customer service from a basic function to a cornerstone of exceptional customer experiences is pivotal for any business. To achieve this, recruiting the right employees is not just beneficial, it is critical. These individuals are the architects of first impressions and the custodians of customer satisfaction. They must possess more than just a script; they should have an intuitive understanding of customer needs, a genuine passion for service, and the ability to empathize and connect on a human level.

The result? A business where customers become advocates, where service transcends transactions, and where each engagement contributes to a lasting relationship.

4. Authentic Self-Promotion:

In professional growth and business development, self-promotion plays a crucial role. It's about strategically spotlighting your successes, and illuminating your accomplishments to peers, potential clients, and the industry at large. However, this isn't simply about boasting—it's about narrating your journey in a genuine and engaging manner. When self-promotion is rooted in authenticity, it transcends vanity and becomes a compelling narrative that inspires, attracts, and educates others. It's a way to showcase the milestones you've achieved and the unique methods that led you there, providing a blueprint for success that others may follow.

5. Community Engagement:

A business that gives back is a business that builds lasting relationships. Engage with your community in ways that align with your values and business goals. (see more about this in a later chapter)

6. Building a Dynamic Team:

Your team is your biggest asset. Invest in recruiting, training, and retaining people who share your vision of excellence.

7. Transparent Pricing:

At our company, we believe that transparency is the cornerstone of trust, particularly in pricing. We proudly display our prices on our website, ensuring every customer knows exactly what to expect without any hidden fees or surprises. This level of openness is more than just a policy—it's a commitment to honesty that gives our customers the peace of mind they deserve when making decisions. By being upfront about costs, we empower our clients, helping them to plan and budget confidently, secure in the knowledge that they are valued and respected partners in our business relationship.

The Journey of Continuous Improvement

This chapter is just the beginning. The following sections will delve deeper into these pillars, offering insights and practical advice on implementing them in your business. Expect stories from my own experiences, lessons learned, and strategies that have proven successful.

Visualizing a New Dawn- Do this on Monday.

Imagine entering your business with a fresh perspective, as if you're the new CEO. What changes would you implement? What strengths would you capitalize on? This exercise can provide invaluable insights and help you approach your business with renewed vigor. ***Do this; I promise it works!***

In the subsequent chapters, we will explore these pillars in-depth, offering you a roadmap to transform your business by competing on excellence, not just price. Let's embark on this journey together, redefining success and creating a legacy of exceptional value.

Before diving into the following chapters, ponder on these questions:

- Reflect on aspects of your business that are done out of habit. How can you innovate these areas?

- Identify recurring complaints or challenges. What changes could address these issues?

- Brainstorm ways to disrupt your industry. Don't limit your thoughts; the more creative, the better.

- Consider how often you seek feedback from clients and employees. How can you create a more effective feedback loop?

- Assess how much time you dedicate to strategic thinking and planning for your business. Set aside regular intervals for this crucial activity.

CHAPTER 3

Embracing Technology

Technology has been a passion of mine for decades. I helped deploy early digital cellular networks in the 1990s and served as an executive rolling out GSM service internationally. Immersing myself in the latest gadgets and innovations energizes me. However, only some people share this enthusiasm. Recently, I heard a technician refer to an iPad as an "iPod thingy," which amused me, given how ubiquitous tablets have become. Though we have different relationships with tech, I'm excited to see what the future brings for both tech enthusiasts like me and the not-so-tech-savvy.

In today's digital world, having intuitive, user-friendly software is crucial for businesses to operate efficiently and provide good customer experiences. Companies rely on software to manage everything from internal systems like HR and accounting to external-facing platforms for sales, marketing, and customer service. Buggy or confusing software leads to wasted time troubleshooting issues, frustrated employees, and dissatisfied customers. On the other hand, robust, easy-to-use software streamlines processes, allows employees to focus on more value-adding tasks and delivers smooth customer journeys. Investing in well-designed, flexible software tailored to a business's needs is essential for reducing costs, enabling innovation and growth, and gaining a competitive edge. With business success so dependent on technology, adopting intuitive, reliable software is a strategic imperative across industries.

In transforming a business, embracing technology is not just an option; it's a necessity. It's akin to learning a new language in a rapidly evolving world. If you're not fluent, you're not just behind – practically invisible.

In 2023, we implemented a robust AI-driven training platform with over 1100 entries. It was a labor of love but well worth the effort. Before this, I was not the type of person who enjoyed systems in day-to-day work, but I have seen the light!

A collaborative approach is the key to successfully integrating technology into your company. Picture this: a diverse group of your team members from different departments and levels of expertise gathered around a large table. They are not just passive participants but active contributors in this technological revolution. Each member is armed with sticky notes, a simple yet effective tool representing various processes and procedures. These notes are then meticulously arranged on a visual wall document, vividly depicting the existing workflow. This is democracy in action, a collective effort to map out the skeleton of your company's processes.

This visual representation is not just a cluster of colorful notes; it's the blueprint for your future. Once these processes are visually laid out, the next step is the digital leap – transferring them into online systems. This is where efficiency meets innovation. At our company, we embraced this change wholeheartedly. Over a week, we digitalized a decade's worth of company history, utilizing not one but eight different kinds of AI. It was a monumental effort, akin to compressing years of evolution into a single, transformative week.

We have always believed in the power of technology. Electronic Key Performance Indicators (KPIs) have been our guiding stars, illuminating the performance path for every team member. These KPIs were not hidden in reports or discussed in hushed tones in boardrooms; they were displayed for all to see, a constant reminder of our collective goals and individual responsibilities.

However, our journey wasn't without its challenges. Holding people accountable to these KPIs was a hurdle we often stumbled over. The root of this challenge was a fear deeply ingrained in our corporate psyche – the fear of losing talent, even if it was subpar. This fear was amplified by the daunting task of finding suitable replacements in a competitive job market.

The turning point came with the advent of our 'Recruiting for a New Generation' process. It was a game-changer, a ray of hope in a seemingly endless talent drought. This new recruiting process, detailed in Chapter 4, streamlined talent acquisition and encouraged us to hold our team accountable. With a reliable system to attract and retain talent, we were no longer shackled by the fear of losing employees. This newfound confidence was reflected in our enhanced ability to implement and enforce systems, driving efficiency and accountability throughout the organization.

Embracing Technology to Enhance Customer Feedback and Employee Empowerment

In the realm of customer service, actively seeking feedback is crucial. Remember, most customers will only spontaneously offer feedback if prompted. However, technology can play a transformative role in this process, making it more effective and insightful.

Integrating technology into the feedback loop does more than just gather opinions; it empowers employees by providing tangible, actionable data. When employees hear customer feedback, especially in a structured and systematic way, it reinforces positive behaviors and identifies areas for improvement. It also fosters open communication and a culture of continuous improvement, bringing to light situations and challenges that might otherwise be overlooked.

For instance, consider the difference between a manager verbally instructing staff to avoid leaving marks on a customer's wall versus using a technology-driven approach. In the latter scenario, we implemented an automatic text-based survey system complemented by follow-up phone calls. This system not only captures customer feedback in real-time but also quantitatively tracks the performance of our technicians against our set expectations.

This feedback is then shared in staff meetings, not just as anecdotal evidence but as concrete data. Managers can now leverage this data to engage in meaningful dialogue with employees when discussing a customer's complaint about a handprint left on their wall. Questions like, "Do you have the necessary cleaning materials on your truck?" or "What steps can we take to ensure we leave the premises spotless?" take on new significance. They transform from hypothetical queries to data-driven discussions, fostering a sense of ownership and responsibility among the staff.

Moreover, this technological approach has significantly improved our management strategies. We use the insights gathered from customer feedback to equip our employees better, such as ensuring that cleaning supplies are always available and instituting mandatory final checks of the work area before leaving a job site.

A Note About Employees

Our journey with employees has been a learning curve. We've encountered many challenges, but technology has been instrumental in refining our hiring and management processes. For instance, we use digital platforms for continuous training and development and for tracking and rewarding desired behaviors. This approach has significantly reduced our employee turnover, which, as studies suggest, can be a substantial hidden cost for businesses.

In our quest for consistency and excellence, technology has been a cornerstone. By setting clear goals, tracking progress digitally, and making necessary adjustments based on data-driven insights, we've managed to identify gaps in our processes and create lasting improvements.

Diving Deeper

Technology remains a key facilitator as we define what 'doing good work' means for our business. Communicating expectations to staff and customers, understanding their feedback, and continuously refining our approaches are all processes augmented by digital tools. We use various software to define roles and responsibilities and envision future positions and growth paths.

1. Incorporate More Diverse Technological Solutions:

During the pandemic, our company barely missed a beat; we have always run as digitally as possible. We no longer have an expensive, clunky phone system; we use an answering service for overflow and after-hours. As they say, necessity is the mother of invention, and 2020 sure tested that old adage in our company and others worldwide.

2. Highlight Employee Training and Development:

Expanding technology aids in employee training and development has provided a more holistic view of its impact on staff empowerment. We use online training, VR glasses, and an AI-driven training program. We now have a total of seven hours of onboarding and training for new employees. The results have been excellent so far!

3. Customer Perspective:

I love all things AI and love my avatars. We have created several "Susan" avatars that my team can use to send personalized video messages to customers to say thanks or any other notes. Scary? You bet! I told my team the first time that if they use my avatar for anything other than quick customer communication, we will have a problem!

Prepare them to meet your expectations, allowing each person to do their job to the best of their ability. What can you take over to create a consistent experience so each staff member can provide the same standard of care to every client? This can include automation tools or delegating tasks to a specific person or people.

Again, it all comes back to setting the goal and then tracking and observing the results. If you want your staff to call a customer back within minutes, what's stopping that from happening now? Set the goal, track it to discover how it is or is not working, adjust, and do it again. Continue to do this until every aspect of *doing good work* matches your expectations.

But how do you track it? Here's an example of a measurement tool we implemented to follow the above four goals. We primarily measure these components through a customer survey automatically sent to every client immediately following their service call. In the survey, we asked if they were called before the technician arrived, if the tech was on time, if we cleaned up after ourselves, and if we solved their problem satisfactorily. This becomes a customer involvement nurture stream and, finally, a phone call.

When it comes to customer feedback, you won't be getting a complete picture of your service if you aren't asking for it. Remember, most people won't leave a review or say what is good or bad unless asked.

A Note About the Technology

In conclusion, integrating technology in managing customer feedback and employee performance is not just about efficiency; it's about empowerment, precision, and fostering a culture of continuous improvement. It's a testament to how technology can be a powerful ally in meeting and exceeding customer expectations and building a motivated, accountable team.

Technology is going to continue to evolve...do you think that AI is going to replace jobs? In some instances, yes I do; in others, I believe I will that employees that KNOW AI will replace jobs! But...can AI replace service and repair technicians? Not for a long, long time....

CHAPTER 4

Modern Networking Strategies for Post-Pandemic Business Success

In the post-pandemic landscape, networking for business has taken on new dimensions. As a business owner, stepping away from day-to-day operations and engaging in effective networking is crucial for establishing trust, forging connections, and building influence. Understanding the evolving nature of networking and adapting to contemporary methods is critical to business growth.

Developing a Networking Strategy

1. Identify Your Ideal Clients: Determine who your target audience is and where they are most likely to be found.

2. Align with Your Mission and Vision: Choose organizations and groups that resonate with your business philosophy.

Evaluating Networking Opportunities; When considering potential networking groups, ask yourself:

- Are my ideal client's members of this group?

- Can I foresee a financial return on my investment?

- What is the anticipated time frame for ROI?

- How much business must I gain to justify the investment?

- What is the required time commitment, and do a team member or I have the bandwidth to dedicate to this?

- Is this within our skill set, or should we consider hiring a dedicated sales or networking specialist?

- Define specific goals for each group (e.g., speaking opportunities, committee leadership, etc.) and assess their feasibility.

More on Speaking:

Effectively communicating about your product or service through public speaking is an invaluable skill in the business world. As a business owner or entrepreneur, becoming a proficient speaker is not just about presenting information; it's about connecting with your audience, building trust, and persuading them of the value of your offer.

Excellent public speaking can elevate your brand, enhance your reputation as an industry leader, and open doors to new opportunities. It allows you to effectively convey your passion, the unique benefits of your products or services, and the story behind your business. These are crucial elements in building lasting relationships with customers, investors, and partners.

In essence, mastering the art of public speaking is an essential component in the toolkit of any successful businessperson, as it directly impacts the perception of your brand and can significantly influence business growth and success.

I have been speaking professionally for about 15 years. It is something that I have always felt comforted to do. I recommend Toastmasters and the National Speakers Association should you want to speak more and need the foundation and direction to get GREAT at your craft.

Networking/ Speaking Suggestions:

Chamber of Commerce: A primary resource for local business development, offering networking events, educational opportunities, and community engagement.

Lead Groups: Organizations like BNI or LeTip provide structured environments for lead exchange personal and professional growth.

Industry-Specific Associations: Join associations relevant to your industry for specialized support, certification opportunities, and lobbying for common causes.

Service Organizations: Groups like Rotary or Kiwanis offer networking with a philanthropic twist, aligning business growth with community service.

Conventions and Conferences: These events provide opportunities for broader exposure, particularly if you can secure a speaking or leadership role.

Key Networking Practices

1. Consistent Participation: Regular attendance is vital. If you can't commit the time, reconsider joining.

2. Active Involvement: Networking is more than mere presence; it's about cultivating relationships.

3. Result Tracking: Monitor the tangible business benefits derived from each group. With the shift towards digital

and hybrid models, consider leveraging online networking platforms and virtual events.

4. Boost Your Visibility: Use your presence in these groups to enhance your reputation as a knowledgeable and reliable business leader.

Embracing Digital Networking

Post-pandemic, digital networking has surged in importance. Incorporate these strategies:

*Virtual Events and Webinar*s: Attend and participate in online events. Consider hosting webinars to establish thought leadership.

Social Media Engagement: Use platforms like LinkedIn to build and nurture professional relationships.

Hybrid Networking Models:

lend in-person and online networking strategies to maximize reach and flexibility.

In the current business climate, networking requires combining traditional methods and innovative digital strategies. By carefully selecting and actively participating in relevant groups and by embracing online networking opportunities, you can expand your business's reach and influence effectively in the post-pandemic world.

Networking, often viewed with mixed feelings, plays a crucial role in business success, as evidenced by my own experience. The essence of networking isn't about grandeur or polish; it's rooted in authenticity and presence. When people know, like, and trust you, they're more inclined to engage in business with you.

This was starkly evident when I temporarily stepped back from our company. In those two years, we witnessed a loss of nearly half a million dollars in business. This downturn was not just a reflection of operational changes but a testament to the impact of personal connections.

My absence was felt by our customer base, underscoring the importance of being visible and accessible. It's not about putting on a show; it's about being genuinely present. People are drawn to do business with someone they feel they know and can trust. This is the core of my networking philosophy – be out there, be accurate, and the connections you foster will translate into tangible business success.

Spark of Awesome, Not on Price Technique:

Track everything and adjust based on the results.

Modernizing KPIs for Networking and Marketing

The Essence of Tracking in Today's Business Landscape

In the dynamic business world, the adage "What gets measured gets managed" holds more truth than ever. The effectiveness of networking and marketing is often obscured, not due to ineffectiveness but rather due to a lack of sophisticated tracking. Embracing Accountability as a core value, it's imperative to view tracking to monitor the performance of activities and gauge their success.

Strategic Planning with Advanced Metrics

Modern business demands a strategic approach to networking and marketing.

1. Defining Target Audience: Identify your target audience through each networking effort. (see more about my target audience)

2. Budgeting Time and Resources Allocate specific time and financial resources with a clear understanding of the expected investment in each networking avenue.

3. Leadership Goals: Set objectives for gaining network leadership roles, and enhancing your influence and visibility. I have been the president of 9 different nonprofits over the years!

4. Advanced Tracking Solutions: Move beyond basic tracking numbers. Utilize CRM systems with advanced analytics capabilities to track interactions and leads. Implement AI-driven tools that can predict and analyze the effectiveness of networking channels in real time.

ROI and KPIs: The Digital Transformation

In the evolving landscape of digital marketing, distinguishing lead sources has indeed become increasingly challenging. The blurring lines between different marketing channels make it difficult to pinpoint exactly where a lead originates. For instance, a potential customer might first encounter your brand on social media, then visit your website, and finally make a call to inquire about services. This multi-channel journey complicates the tracking process.

Previously, methods like using multiple tracking numbers offered a solution, but as you've experienced, these are less effective. The integration of various platforms means that traditional tracking methods need help to keep up with the nuanced paths customers take before they convert.

Marketers are indeed striving to develop more sophisticated tracking mechanisms. The focus is shifting towards comprehensive analytics tools that can track a customer's journey across multiple touchpoints and platforms. These tools aim to provide a more holistic view of the customer journey, capturing interactions from initial exposure to final conversion.

For your business, exploring advanced analytics solutions that offer cross-channel tracking and attribution modeling might be beneficial. These tools can help in understanding how different marketing efforts contribute to conversions, even when the customer journey is complex and multi-faceted. By gaining clearer insights into which channels and campaigns are most effective, you can allocate resources more efficiently and tailor your strategies to better engage with your target audience, like the

'Bougie Betties'.

Digital Tracking Tools:

Use digital tools for tracking networking efforts. Implement systems that auto-populate client information based on the lead source, ensuring seamless integration with your digital marketing strategies.

-ROI Thresholds: Establish clear ROI thresholds. For instance, if a $1,000 investment in a networking group doesn't yield at least $2,000 in leads or business, reconsider its viability.

-Data-Driven Decisions: Utilize data analytics to understand the average client value and determine how many engagements are needed to achieve desired returns. This data-driven approach should guide investment decisions in networking and marketing activities.

Embracing Technology for Efficiency

Paperless and Digital Operations: Ensure all operations, including networking tracking, are digital and paperless. Utilize cloud-based systems for real-time access to essential data like KPIs, client information, and operational metrics.

Mobile Management: Leverage mobile technology to remotely monitor business activities, ensuring constant connectivity and informed decision-making.

Employee Engagement in Networking

Role-Specific Networking: Delegate networking responsibilities based on role suitability. Management and sales roles are typically more effective at networking due to their outcome-oriented nature and accountability.

Training and Support: Provide necessary training and support to staff involved in networking. This includes guidance on interaction, expectation setting, and feedback mechanisms.

Compensation and Incentive Structures: Develop compensation models that incentivize networking results for sales personnel.

The Future of Networking: AI and Automation

AI in Networking: Explore AI solutions that can recommend optimal networking groups and predict the success rate based on industry trends and past performance data.

Automated Feedback and Referral Systems: Implement automated systems for collecting feedback and referrals, ensuring a constant loop of information that feeds into refining networking strategies.

Conclusion: Leveraging Data for Networking Success

Actionable Insights: Use the collected data to make informed decisions. Regularly review KPIs to assess the effectiveness of networking efforts.

Continuous Improvement: Networking and marketing are dynamic processes. Regularly update your strategies based on the latest market trends, technological advancements, and performance data.

Reflective Questions for Deeper Analysis

1. Evaluation of Past Efforts: Assess previous networking strategies. What worked, what didn't, and why?

2. Future Endeavors: Identify potential networking groups or platforms. How will they align with your business goals?

3. Result Tracking: Determine the metrics and tools you will use to track your networking efforts. Consider AI and data analytics tools for more nuanced insights.

4. Team Involvement: Decide who is best suited for networking roles in your organization. How will you support and measure their efforts?

5. Revisit Initial Assessments: Regularly return to the foundational questions about each networking effort to ensure alignment with overall business objectives.

Modernizing your approach to tracking and evaluating networking and marketing efforts can transform these activities into strategic assets, driving growth and enhancing your business's competitive edge.

How will you track your results?

CHAPTER 5

Recruiting for a New Generation

As an entrepreneur, I faced a challenge that is all too common in the business world: the struggle to find and hire the right people. This frustration wasn't just about filling positions but about discovering individuals who shared our vision, passion, and drive. Traditional hiring methods fell short, and I knew something had to change. This realization marked the beginning of an 18-month journey of exploration, learning, and, ultimately, innovation in recruitment.

My quest led me to the heart of the matter – the young, vibrant workforce shaping the future of business. I embarked on a mission to understand their aspirations, values, and what they sought in their professional lives. This wasn't a superficial survey but an in-depth exploration involving numerous interviews with young professionals from diverse backgrounds. I listened to their stories, understood their perspectives, and started seeing the world of work through their eyes.

This process was transformative. It became clear that the conventional recruitment playbook needed to be updated and more effective in resonating with the new generation. Their expectations were different, their motivations more varied, and their relationship with technology more intimate. As an AI super user and a leader in a fast-growing Inc 5000 company, I realized that leveraging technology, especially AI, could revolutionize how we approach hiring.

This introduction sets the stage for the subsequent chapter, where I unveil the "Recruiting for a New-Generation" program. This innovative approach is not just a set of techniques; it's a paradigm shift in recruitment, aligning with the new workforce's values, desires, and expectations. The journey from a frustrated entrepreneur to a trailblazer in recruitment has been arduous but rewarding, and I'm excited to share these insights and strategies with you.

Understanding the Modern Candidate

During my 18-month journey of enlightenment, where I sought deeper understanding and insights into the workforce of today, I consistently asked every young interviewee a set of crucial questions. These questions were aimed at uncovering what the new generation values in their professional life and how employers can adapt to meet these expectations. The insights gained from these questions were invaluable in shaping a more progressive, understanding, and employee-centric workplace culture. Here are the key questions I explored:

What do you look for in an Employer?

Understanding what qualities or attributes in an employer are most appealing to young professionals.

What is Important to you when selecting a job?

Identifying the factors that play a significant role in their decision-making process for job selection.

How can an employer make you feel valued?

They are gaining insight into what actions or policies make employees feel appreciated and recognized in their workplace.

What are your job priorities?

Discovering what aspects of a job hold the most importance for them, such as work-life balance, career growth, or job security.

These questions not only helped in understanding the evolving dynamics of the employer-employee relationship but also provided a roadmap for creating a more fulfilling and engaging work environment.

The landscape of recruitment has evolved dramatically. To attract top talent today, it's crucial to first understand what the new generation of job seekers is looking for. They are not just seeking a job; they are looking for a role that aligns with their values and offers a sense of purpose. They want to be seen as individuals, not just another name on a resume.

Revolutionizing Job Ads

Gone are the days when traditional job ads would suffice. In today's digital era, the most effective strategy is to employ reverse lookup tools on various job boards. This proactive approach allows you to reach potential candidates directly, tapping into a pool of talent that's fresh and often highly motivated.

The Magic Hour: Timing Your Search

Timing plays a critical role in recruitment. Sunday afternoons have emerged as the 'magic hour' for sourcing candidates. Why? If employees are frustrated with their current roles, they often spend the weekend reflecting and updating their resumes. By Sunday, they're ripe for new opportunities. This is the time to dive into job databases, filtering candidates from the last three days, to find those fresh, eager prospects.

Personalized Engagement

Once you've identified potential candidates, the key is personalization. Automated systems may speed up the process, but nothing beats a personalized email that speaks directly to the candidate's skills and experience. Furthermore, including a video message from the hiring manager (a must in larger companies) adds a human touch that resonates with younger job seekers.

They want to know who they will be working with, not just the company they'll be joining. Now hear this, this video needs to be RAW, nothing fancy...au contraire, you want it to be gritty and real. I know that some people reading this may have fancy video set ups and maybe even a studio...don't do it! Make your video more like you are meeting a new networking friend for coffee! DO NOT DELEGATE to the HR Department!

Here is an example of mine: https://youtu.be/dhj1QDJLyI4

Social Media Presence

Be mindful of your social media presence. Candidates will often conduct their own research on potential employers. Ensure your social channels reflect the values and culture of your company, as these platforms are now an integral part of your organization's public face.

The Power of Immediate Communication

Upon receiving a response, it's crucial to engage with the candidate through their preferred communication channels, such as texting or email. This helps in setting up a video interview promptly. In a competitive job market, where candidates may be juggling multiple interviews, swift and effective communication can be the difference between securing top talent and losing them to a competitor.

Post-Interview Connection

After the interview, sending a personalized video email can significantly impact the candidate's experience. This message should recap the interview, highlight what stood out about the candidate, and, if applicable, reiterate the job offer. This approach reinforces the personal connection and shows genuine interest in the candidate as an individual.

Onboarding and Integration

Once a new employee is onboarded, leveraging systems like Gusto for payroll and integrating them into your learning management system (as discussed in Chapter 2) is essential. Encouraging new hires to interact with different departments helps them understand the company's workings and ethos. Demonstrating your company's commitment to customer satisfaction and a positive work environment from day one is crucial for long-term engagement and retention.

One of the most striking revelations is the human connection they crave in the workplace. This generation isn't just looking for a job or a company to work for; they seek a deeper, more personal connection with their employers. They want to work for someone who genuinely sees, knows, and appreciates them. It's not just about a paycheck or a title; it's about being part of something where they feel valued and understood personally.

Another significant shift is in the attitude towards mental health. Unlike previous generations, where mental health was often a taboo subject, shrouded in silence and stigma, today's young workforce is refreshingly open about it. They talk about their mental health needs without shame, embracing their vulnerabilities as a normal part of life. They are not hesitant to request time off for mental health reasons, recognizing the importance of mental well-being for overall productivity and happiness.

This paradigm shift presents a unique challenge and opportunity for employers. We must adapt our workplaces to be more welcoming, inclusive, and empathetic to attract and retain this new generation of workers. We need to create environments where young employees feel proud and excited to come to work, feel their mental health is taken seriously, and their individuality is respected.

In practical terms, this means:

1. ***Fostering Personal Connections***: Building a culture where management and staff engage in meaningful ways beyond work-related tasks. This could be through team-building activities, regular check-ins, or creating spaces for casual interactions.

2. ***Promoting Mental Health Awareness:*** Actively incorporating mental health support within the company policies. This could include mental health days, access to counseling services, and training for managers to recognize and sensitively respond to mental health issues.

3. ***Creating Inclusive Policies***: Developing workplace policies that recognize and celebrate diversity in all its forms. This includes not just ethnic and gender diversity but also diversity in thoughts, backgrounds, and experiences.

4. ***Encouraging Open Dialogue***: Creating an environment where employees feel safe to express their ideas, concerns, and suggestions without fear of judgment or retribution.

5. ***Offering Flexibility***: Providing flexible work options that recognize the varying needs of employees, whether it's flexible hours, the option to work remotely, or understanding family obligations.

6. ***Investing in Employee Development***: Demonstrating a commitment to employees' personal and professional growth through training, mentoring, and clear paths for advancement.

By embracing these strategies, we can create workplaces that attract the new generation of workers and foster a culture of respect, innovation, and shared success. It's about moving from traditional, rigid work models to more human-centric approaches that value individuality and well-being. This is the future of work, and it's a future that promises to be more fulfilling for everyone involved.

Embracing the Future: A New Approach to Hiring step by step.

1. ***Understanding the New Workforce***: Today's generation values flexibility, work-life balance, and personal and professional growth opportunities. They seek employers who are bosses, mentors, and enablers of their ambitions.

2. ***Leveraging AI and Technology***: As an AI super user, I recognized the untapped potential of AI in streamlining and enhancing the recruitment process. By integrating AI tools, I was able to analyze vast amounts of data, predict candidate success more accurately, and create a more efficient and engaging recruitment experience.

3. ***Cultivating an Appealing Corporate Culture***: The research highlighted the importance of a positive and inclusive work environment. I focused on building a culture that resonates with the new generation's values – collaborative, innovative, and socially responsible.

4. ***Innovative Recruitment Techniques***: Moving beyond traditional job postings, I implemented creative strategies like engaging video presentations and interactive digital platforms to attract and retain the best talent. This approach showcased my company's dynamic nature and appealed to the tech-savvy new generation.

5. ***Focus on Personal Development***: Recognizing the aspiration for growth, I developed programs focusing on continuous learning and skill enhancement, aligning with the career goals of the new workforce.

6. ***An Emphasis on Social Responsibility***: In line with the new generation's values, I ensured that my company's ethos and actions reflected a solid commitment to social responsibility and community involvement.

The Impact and Outcomes

Reflecting on my journey, I realize how stepping away from our company for two years led to significant challenges upon my return. I found myself during a mess, necessitating a complete overhaul - stripping everything down to the studs and starting anew. This process meant that many of our existing employees wouldn't fit into the new vision we had for the company. The culture of accountability and pride in work had dissipated in my absence, and it was evident that everyone was just floating around.

This was a major lesson for me. Since the beginning of this year, we've hired 11 new people using the "Recruiting for a New Generation" process. Each one of them has shared that they felt a connection to me, which was a significant factor in their decision to join our team. This new approach to business was foreign to me. Coming from a background in a Fortune 10 company and working in British-led countries, I was accustomed to a very different way of conducting business. The transition was a rude awakening, but I am grateful for it. It has made me the best leader I've ever been.

Being open about my own deficiencies and challenges, including dealing with a traumatic brain injury, ADHD, and the aftermath of a physically active lifestyle, has been a part of this journey. It's made me more vulnerable and relatable, enhancing my ability to lead with empathy and understanding. This experience has not just improved my leadership skills but has also profoundly enriched my perspective.

Moving Forward: Continuous Evolution

The journey continues. The business landscape and the workforce's needs and expectations are constantly changing. My commitment is to stay at the forefront of these changes, continuously evolving and adapting my recruitment strategies. By staying true to the core values of innovation, empathy, and excellence, I aim to lead by example, inspiring others to embrace the future of recruitment.

This chapter encapsulates my journey and the innovative strategies in recruitment.

CHAPTER 6

Deliver Mind-Blowing Customer Service

You hear a lot about customers, avatars target markets, etc.... We really went deep on this in the last year. We have come up with three top initiatives one: our number one demographic customer is a woman in her 40s 50s and beyond and wants top-notch service and also a company that's run by another woman! Two we have online pricing I know that sounds absurd in our business but it's true that's what we do right on the website! And online scheduling... I don't know about you, but for me, I will bypass Business if I can't schedule online. I like to schedule when I'm thinking about it and not between 9 to 5 Monday through Friday.

Competing based on price is a misguided strategy that can hinder the growth and sustainability of your business. Instead, the focus should be on differentiating through superior customer service. It's crucial to understand that regardless of the number of competitors or the prevalence of similar skill sets, what sets your business apart is its unique value proposition. When considering pricing, it should reflect your business goals and the distinct value you provide, not merely a response to market competition.

Innovative businesses today are shifting from traditional competitive strategies to creating distinct customer experiences. This involves understanding your clients' needs deeply and tailoring your services to exceed their expectations, thereby crafting memorable and impactful customer experiences.

For instance, our journey to becoming a renowned customer service company, evidenced during our recognition as a finalist for the Better Business Bureau Torch Award in 2016, underscores the effectiveness of this approach.

The judges' acknowledgment:

"Sunshine is a customer service company providing plumbing and heating services."

This statement affirmed our commitment to prioritizing customer service over price competition. Our innovative approach to customer service is encapsulated in the 'Sunshine 12 Points of Love', a set of principles that guide our interactions with clients and set a high standard for our team. These principles are not just unique to our industry; they are adaptable and can be a model for businesses across various sectors. Here's a glimpse into how we've revolutionized customer service

Our Human Side

We believe in the power of the human connection. That's why, after completing a service, we don't rely solely on the digital thank-you; we make it a point to reach out with a phone call within 48 hours. This isn't just a courtesy call; it's an authentic check-in to ensure satisfaction. We recognize that issues—like an overlooked smudge or a loose fixture—might only come to light once we've left. Our aim is to catch these small moments of discontent before they become silent grievances that erode trust.

Reflect on your own experiences—those instances where a service fell short, not disastrously, but enough that you decided not to return. It's in these stories, often untold to the service provider, where loyalty is lost. Our proactive approach seeks to give voice to the silent, to convert detractors into supporters through the simple, yet profound act of listening.

Continuing the conversation, our monthly email newsletters serve not as mere sales flurries but as a treasure trove of value for our clients. They're packed with specials, sure, but also with nuggets of wisdom on making savvy choices or understanding the nuts and bolts of home maintenance. It's a monthly reminder that we're here, not just when things go awry, but as a constant source of support.

But what about the newsletter seen through the lens of customer service? It would be a vessel carrying not just promotions, but also stories of service beyond expectation, insights into the people behind the company, and opportunities for our clients to engage with us on a deeper level.

And then, there's the art of the Thank You note. In an era of instant messaging, a handwritten note is a rare gem that signals care and appreciation. It's a simple gesture, but one that resonates in the heart of the receiver. We take pride in sending out personalized cards that stand out in a sea of digital communication, an unexpected delight that sets us apart from the rest.

Gift-giving, too, is part of our ethos. Not as a loud proclamation but as a subtle gesture of thanks for placing trust in our services. We've refined the art of gifting, finding that sweet spot where thoughtfulness meets surprise. And when we fall short, we don't hide—we send a 'Boo-Boo Gift,' a tangible apology that speaks louder than words.

Our service extends beyond the human members of the household. By keeping dog biscuits on hand, we acknowledge and honor every part of the family we serve, including the four-legged ones.

In extreme circumstances, we've been known to go to extraordinary lengths, like providing hotel accommodations when a fix isn't immediate. It's a bold move, but it's these stories of unparalleled service that leave a lasting impression.

So now, I ask you to ponder your service landscape. How does your customer service stack up? Is it the heart of your company? Take a moment to consider how you can infuse even more humanity into your service, to not just be a provider, but a partner to your clients. What immediate action can you take? What long-term strategies can you weave into the very fabric of your company culture to ensure that customer service isn't just a department, but a defining feature of your brand?

Remember, in a world rapidly moving towards automation, the human touch is the hallmark of timeless customer service. It's not just about being good; it's about being memorable.

These principles are not just a checklist; they embody our commitment to exceptional service. By openly sharing and advocating these principles, we set a high bar for our team and communicate our dedication to outstanding service to our clients. This approach is a testament to the power of customer service in creating a distinguished and successful business, transcending traditional price-based competition.

Incorporating Artificial Intelligence (AI) into your business strategy can significantly enhance your ability to deliver superior customer service and achieve better results. AI technologies offer innovative ways to understand, predict, and meet client needs more efficiently and effectively. Here are some ideas for leveraging AI to elevate your customer service:

Since the technology is moving so fast stay tuned for more updates from us! And now...AI for all of us...

1. AI-Powered Customer Insights:

- Use AI algorithms to analyze customer data and feedback.

- Gain deeper insights into customer preferences, behaviors, and trends.

- Tailor your services and communications based on these insights to meet individual customer needs better.

2. Chatbots and Virtual Assistants:

- Implement AI-driven chatbots on your website and social media platforms.

- Provide instant, 24/7 responses to common customer inquiries, improving responsiveness.

- Use chatbots for appointment scheduling, reminders, or providing information about services and promotions.

3. Personalized Customer Experiences:

- Employ AI to create personalized experiences for each customer.

- Customize communication and offers based on individual customer interactions and history.

- Use predictive analytics to anticipate customer needs and proactively offer solutions.

4. Automated Follow-up and Engagement: (when appropriate!! Many scenarios still require a person!)

- Utilize AI tools for automated email and message follow-ups.

- Ensure consistent and timely communication without overwhelming your staff.

- Analyze engagement data to refine the timing and content of follow-ups.

5. AI-Enhanced Customer Feedback Collection:

- Use AI tools to gather and analyze customer feedback efficiently.

- Implement sentiment analysis to understand customer emotions and satisfaction levels.

- Use these insights to make data-driven improvements to your service offerings.

6. Efficiency in Operations:

- AI can optimize scheduling, logistics, and inventory management.

- Implement smart routing for service calls to minimize travel time and maximize efficiency.

- Use predictive maintenance for equipment, reducing downtime and ensuring reliability.

7. Training and Support for Employees:

- Leverage AI for training programs using virtual simulations and personalized learning paths.

- Provide AI-assisted support tools for employees to access information quickly while on service calls.

- Use AI to analyze performance data, helping employees improve their skills and service delivery.

8. Voice Recognition and Natural Language Processing:

- Incorporate voice recognition for hands-free operation and accessibility.

- Use natural language processing to understand and respond to customer inquiries more naturally and effectively.

- Integrating these AI-driven strategies can significantly enhance your customer service capabilities. AI helps understand and meet customer needs more effectively, streamlines operations, improves employee performance, and contributes to a more sophisticated and customer-centric business model.

Integrating AI avatars and a world-class onboarding and training program can significantly elevate the efficiency and consistency of your customer service. Here's an expanded approach that includes these elements:

1. AI Avatars for Client Communication:

- Employ AI avatars to send personalized messages and updates to clients.

- These avatars can provide a more engaging and interactive communication, enhancing the customer experience.

- Utilize avatars for delivering service reminders, updates on ongoing work, and even gathering feedback.

2. Customized Onboarding with AI Assistance:

- Develop an AI-enhanced onboarding program for new clients.

- Use AI to personalize the onboarding process based on each client's specific needs and preferences.

- Automate the collection of essential client information and preferences, ensuring a smooth initiation into your services.

3. World-Class AI-Driven Training Program:

- Implement an AI-based employee training system, ensuring consistency and excellence in service delivery.

- Use AI to customize training modules based on individual employee performance and learning pace.

- Incorporate virtual reality (VR) or augmented reality (AR) for immersive training experiences, especially for technical and practical skills.

4. Consistent Service Delivery:

- Ensure uniform service standards across the organization through AI-monitored protocols.

- Use AI to analyze service delivery patterns and identify areas for improvement.

- Implement AI-driven checklists and reminders for employees to maintain high service standards in every interaction.

5. Proactive Client Engagement with AI Avatars:

- Utilize AI avatars for proactive client engagement, such as offering tips, updates on new services, or educational content related to your services.

- Program avatars to recognize client milestones or special occasions, adding a personalized touch to your service.

6. Feedback and Improvement Loop:

- Employ AI tools to collect and analyze feedback from clients post-interaction continuously.

- Use this data to refine your service offerings and customer interaction strategies.

- Allow AI systems to autonomously suggest and implement minor improvements, keeping your services dynamic and responsive to client needs.

7. AI for Predictive Client Needs Analysis:

- Leverage AI to predict clients' future needs based on their history and interactions.

- Proactively seek solutions or suggestions, enhancing client satisfaction and loyalty.

By incorporating AI avatars for client communication and a sophisticated AI-driven onboarding and training program, your business can offer unparalleled consistency and quality in customer service. This approach streamlines operations and personalizes the client experience, ensuring that your services stand out in a competitive market.

Spark of Awesome, Not on Price Technique:

Maximize Reviews

Incorporating a focus on customer reviews and leveraging AI to enhance client engagement can transform your approach to customer service. Here's a revised version of the section with these elements integrated:

Maximizing the Impact of Customer Reviews:

Imagine the powerful impression your company could make if just 10% of your customers left 4- or 5-star reviews. Take your average weekly sales and calculate 10% of that figure – the number of positive reviews you accumulate over a year could significantly surpass your competitors. We emphasize the importance of studies in our follow-up process. Reflect on your client follow-up strategies: Are you actively seeking feedback and reviews? If not, it's time to establish a system for engaging every customer in this crucial process.

Mandatory Review Collection for Team Incentives:

Our team members are encouraged to gather at least five customer reviews to qualify for bonuses or promotions. This practice boosts our online presence and ensures continuous feedback for service improvement.

Follow-Up by Phone Within Two Days:

Here is a place NOT to use AI! This needs to be you!

Beyond automated emails post-service, we make personalized calls to clients two days after job completion. This step is crucial for uncovering any overlooked issues, such as unnoticed handprints or loose fixtures, and addressing them proactively. This approach retains clients and transforms passive customers into active promoters of our services.

Are you ready to dive in deeper?

Let's take some time to dive into the questions we asked earlier in the chapter.

What are you already doing as part of your customer service that can be better documented and shared?

What's your company tagline or motto? Does it clearly communicate your overall objective?

What systems, software, apps or automation might you implement to help improve your customer experience?

What do you have in place to follow up with 100% of your clients? What needs to change to make this happen?

What 'wow' can be implemented for when you make a mistake?

CHAPTER 7

Shamelessly Self-Promote

Mastering the Art of Shameless Self-Promotion

In the business growth journey, mastering shameless self-promotion is a pivotal chapter, especially after establishing a foundation of exceptional customer service. The harmony between these two aspects can significantly amplify your business's voice in a crowded market. When your service is extraordinary, self-praise isn't just noise; it becomes a chorus, joined by the representatives of satisfied customers. This synergy is central to competing on excellent, not just on price.

Self-promotion, often viewed with hesitation, especially among those who entered the business with an aversion to sales and marketing, is in fact a vital instrument of success. Let's debunk the myth: if you're in business, you're in the business of marketing yourself. It's not about being brash; it's about being boldly authentic about your values.

To illustrate, let me share a lesson from Aunt Frankie, a relative who embodies the spirit of confident self-assurance. During a financial low in my career, Aunt Frankie offered me not sympathy but a Jersey-style kickstart: "Susan, polish off those brass balls you have and go make a sale. You're a phenomenal salesperson, a great coach – go make it happen." That epitomized straightforward motivation, the kind I now channel in my leadership and advice.

Embracing shameless self-promotion isn't about straying from your ethical compass or personal alignment. Rather, it's about owning your success and the value you deliver. It's about shifting the mindset from humility to pride in your accomplishments and service. This perspective turns self-promotion into a mission, a joy, rather than a burden. It's about shouting from the mountaintops because you believe in the impact you're making.

Particularly for women in business, who often grapple with modesty, breaking free from self-imposed limitations is crucial. Reflect on these questions to assess your readiness to self-promote:

- Do you always carry business cards, ready to share your story?

- Are you comfortable with your elevator pitch able to engage anyone within a three-foot radius?

- Do you feel any shame about your business, and if so, what's the root cause?

- Is your hesitation linked to misconceptions about money or sales?

- What's your sales process and marketing strategy?

- Have you considered using awards to enhance your brand's visibility?

A profound shift occurs when pride in your work overshadows humility. This isn't arrogance; it's confidence born from the knowledge that you provide something of real value. Our marketing strategy embraces this concept, leveraging awards as a testament to our excellence. These accolades are more than trophies; they affirm our commitment to outstanding service and innovation.

In conclusion, transforming your business narrative through shameless self-promotion is not just about being heard – it's about being recognized for your excellence and impact. This chapter is about embracing and broadcasting your successes, knowing that what you offer is not just a service or product but a contribution to your clients' lives and the broader community.

Take inspiration from my mentor, Aunt Frankie, a beacon of confidence and clarity. She once told me during a challenging phase, "Susan, it's time to shine. You have the skills, the knowledge, and the drive. Now, go out there and show the world what you're made of." This Jersey-style, no-nonsense encouragement is the essence of the mindset needed for self-promotion.

Self-promotion is about embracing your achievements and the impact of your work. It's about understanding that marketing your business is not just necessary but a responsibility to those who could benefit from your services. Here are some reflective questions to help you evaluate and enhance your self-promotion strategy:

- Do you carry your business story with you, ready to share at a moment's notice?
- Are you leveraging the power of digital platforms to showcase your brand's story and values?
- How do you react to opportunities for visibility? Do you embrace them or shy away?

- Are your marketing strategies aligned with current trends and customer behaviors post-pandemic?

- Have you explored awards and recognitions that are relevant and prestigious in today's market?

Embracing the art of self-promotion is about moving beyond traditional humility and stepping into a space where your business's voice is heard, respected, and sought after. For example, our approach to leveraging awards has evolved. We target recognitions that resonate with our core values and echo the changing market dynamics. These awards are not mere accolades but a testament to our adaptability, resilience, and commitment to excellence in a rapidly changing business world.

This chapter is a call to action to position your brand boldly and strategically in the marketplace. It's about understanding that your voice, story, and achievements are not just worth sharing but are essential components of your business's growth and influence in a post-pandemic world. This is your moment to step into the spotlight with confidence and purpose, showcasing the unique value you bring to your clients and your industry.

Are you ready to dive in deeper?

Let's take some time to dive into the questions we asked earlier in the chapter.

Write out your "elevator pitch" for the Three-Foot Rule:

Do you have a mindset issue about money or greed that needs to be addressed?

What additional skills do you need to feel truly confident in business? (i.e. sales, process, strategy, etc.)

What type of award would matter to your client?

What type of award matters to your company and staff?

What award(s) can you apply for to increase your exposure?

CHAPTER 8

Give Back to the Community

Numerous articles have been written on the value that companies get for community involvement and philanthropy. They cite studies showing that businesses with a give-back mentality have a positive financial impact on their bottom line. Most companies that desire to give back don't do it for this purpose, but it is a bit like Fate giving a reward for your generosity and charity. But there is another reason for giving back that you may not have considered: Millennials and Gen Z.

Millennials are the largest generation since the Baby Boomers, and they are currently entering the workforce. While there are endless jokes about how frustrating they can be, the truth is, as employers, we need to understand how to work with them if we will have a successful workforce. Working for a socially responsible company is one known priority of Millennials.

Spark of Awesome, Not on Price Technique:

Be a Thought Leader

So, as we looked at hiring, we need to understand what type of culture is attractive to the types of employees we want. Sometimes, this means getting creative – for us that meant creating more awareness around the worker shortage we have in our industry and finding ways to circumvent it, such as:

Video Plumber® – Allows us to work smarter by creating an opportunity for technicians with the skill, but potentially not the physical ability, to provide a quote. We see this product as an opportunity to help disabled employees, such as veterans, with plumbing and/or HVAC skills to work from a desk, rather than in the field. They can write quotes and order parts for another technician to complete the work, saving time and money.

TedX – This platform allowed me, along with two other successful women in the trades who I've met along the way, to spread the word more publicly about the skills gap, encouraging women to consider the trades. TedX gave me a platform to share about this topic in a much broader way. If you haven't considered it before, I encourage you to look into the opportunities in your area.

Creating a Culture – I've mentioned before that we built into our culture the idea of corporate give-back. As a company, we volunteer at a local food bank, and employees are encouraged to tell us about situations where we may be of service. This includes Habitat for Humanity projects and any needs from their church or other organizations they participate in.

Sustainability – This is a hot topic for young people, but is even more critical to many Coloradans who want to keep the state beautiful. My husband, William Frew, formerly installed solar and is an avid rock climber. He brings this passion for the environment into our work practices. The use of technology and thoughtful management practices have allowed our company to embrace sustainability. The use of an iPad will enable us to eliminate paper invoices or work orders, all billing and filing is also paperless, and GPS units on our trucks provide better gas efficiency. We also practice recycling of scrap metal, including water heaters and other plumbing and heating supplies. In addition, we have a company-wide practice of always bringing plumbing up to code and encouraging the use of the highest efficiencies put in place by the National Appliance Energy Conservation Act.

When thinking about community give-back, consider WHO you want as employees and what's important to them, then build a culture that provides that. Most employees will follow the leader, so if animals are essential to you, they will likely be critical to your employees as well. If you choose to give back to the community with animal-related charities, prospective employees who value that will be more likely to work with you. Think about this when you choose how to give back and what types of people will then attract as employees.

Culture includes aligning policies, procedures, KPIs... everything towards the goals you want the company to achieve and work towards. Too often, ideals are expressed in a vision or mission statement but aren't genuinely demonstrated in the day-to-day workings of the business. Again, this can come back to the unwillingness to change. However, to have a successful company, you must examine where there is misalignment and what type of culture you are creating.

Initially, our give-back culture consisted of putting peanut butter and jelly sandwiches on every truck for the technicians to hand out to homeless people. We now laugh at the number of smashed sandwiches we would find during inventory. After all, our technicians weren't driving around looking for homeless people, they were working. We decided instead to put dog biscuits on the trucks. These were non-perishable and could be given to our clients' dogs which were a lot easier to come by. We also decided to start serving at the food bank every quarter which gave us a direct connection to those we wished to serve without the stink of rotten sandwiches in our vans.

Some other examples of community give back that set us apart include:

- Performing repair and maintenance for an elderly woman on a fixed income
- Donating 20 hours of labor and supplies to restore the home of a family who lost their dad to a dangerous gas leak that made their home unlivable.
- Fixing leaks and restoring water service to a women's victim center.

We've talked in another chapter about shameless self-promotion, and there are times when we've let the media know the types of work we do for the community. However, there are other times we keep it more discreet, sharing it in specific situations, like this book and awards applications, or even just with our team. It often has to do with the sensitivity of the service. For example, it would be unsafe to disclose the location of a women's victim center or further disrupt a family who has experienced tremendous loss. However, consider the times and types of ways you can promote your community service to position you as a Spark of Awesome, Not on Price. This brings us to my favorite community give back that we offer.

The Birth of Thiftinista

I am often complimented on my attire while networking, speaking, or even out in public. People ask me where I bought it, and most people are surprised when I tell them how little I spent by purchasing my look at a thrift store. The truth is, I am a recessionista. Before the recession, I shopped in high-end stores. Style and fashion are important to me, so I know about designers and brands. I refused to give up my favorites even when I didn't have the income to support buying them new. But because of my experience, I could find my favorite brands and styles easily.

Well, one day I was conversing with my marketing company – Crazy Good Marketing – about an idea I had to offer a bus trip to thrift stores. She liked the idea and said I should have Sunshine sponsor it, therefore highlighting the company to our demographic, which was made up of 80% women. Thriftinista became a public relations stunt designed to get in front of our target market – women – and offer something of value to our community – shopping at local thrift stores.

Sunshine collaborated with another marketing power partner, CampExperience™ Network, a networking and philanthropic organization we are involved with. A chartered bus was lent to us, free of charge, and women lined up to purchase bus tickets for the day-long event. The participants met at Sunshine for a light breakfast and were offered coupons for Sunshine's plumbing and heating services. They then loaded the bus and received a short talk featuring shopping tips and an opportunity to create a plan. I assisted them with shopping and getting the best deal at four thrift stores that day. The thrift stores benefited from the sales, but they also received a portion of the fares the women paid for the bus trip. A catered box lunch was served on the bus and the feedback we received after that first event was phenomenal. We have continued to offer these bus trips and have donated over $10,000 for Goodwill, Rotary Club, and Stout Street Residential Treatment Facility in the last year (2018).

A Note About Employees

When you create a culture of the community give-back, it will permeate your entire company for the better. In another chapter, you will hear about our benefits package, which is very attractive to our employees - a way to give back to the community by creating a valuable employment culture. Community give back, along with some of the crazy benefits we offer employees, aren't known to them when they are hired, but instead, they experience it while working with us. Those who don't align with our values will move on, and we are okay with this.

Too often I hear business owners settle for employees who can perform a specific task, but don't fit the company's values simply because they don't want to find a replacement. At our company, we'd rather have the right type of employee, instead of just any employee. Part of community give back is having employees who are on board with it, and also experience it themselves. You will see an increase in morale if employees are treated as well as any community service you perform.

Are you ready to dive in deeper?

- Let's take some time to dive into the questions we asked earlier in the chapter.

- What ways can you establish yourself as a thought leader in your industry?

- What organizations can you support in your community?

- What ways can you give back in ways that are meaningful to your target market?

- What give back opportunities do your employees value

CHAPTER 9

Create a Star Team

Innovative Employee Engagement and Smart Hiring in the Modern Era In today's dynamic business environment, where technology and AI are reshaping the landscape, it's essential to adopt progressive strategies for employee engagement and smart hiring. Our approach to managing our team and recruiting talent is designed not just to keep up with the times but to set new standards in the industry.

Modern Employee Benefits and Engagement:

1. No On-Call Hours:

We've revolutionized the traditional service industry norm of rotating on-call shifts. Our team enjoys a healthy work-life balance, with no after-hours work. We leverage technology and AI solutions to provide emergency support, ensuring our clients receive prompt assistance while our technicians spend quality time with their families.

2. Unlimited Personal Time Off (PTO):

Our employees can access unlimited unpaid PTO. We trust our team's judgment and have found that this policy rarely gets abused. This level of flexibility contributes significantly to employee satisfaction and retention.

3. Flexible Scheduling with Remote Work Options:

With our digital infrastructure, our team members can opt for flexible schedules, including remote work options, aligning with our commitment to work-life balance and technological innovation.

4. LegalShield and Financial Wellness Programs:

We offer LegalShield to provide employees with legal support and advice, ensuring their focus remains on work. Additionally, we encourage financial wellness through programs like Financial Peace University, supporting our team in building a solid financial foundation.

5. AI-Enhanced Training and Development:

Our world-class onboarding and training programs are integrated with AI-driven tools, providing personalized learning experiences and ensuring consistency in skill development.

6. Rewarding Review-Driven Performance:

Emphasizing the importance of customer feedback, we have implemented an AI-based system where employees must attain a minimum number of positive reviews to qualify for bonuses or promotions. This system not only incentivizes excellent service but also fosters a culture of continuous improvement.

7. Surprise Perks and Comprehensive Benefits:

From unexpected treats like company outings to comprehensive health insurance and paid volunteer days, we ensure our benefits package is as innovative as our business approach.

Revolutionizing Retention for a New Generation:

Our recruitment process is tailored to meet the challenges of a new generation of workers. We use AI-driven tools and techniques to identify candidates with the required technical skills and align with our company culture and values.

1. Visual Skill Tests:

Developed by our team, these tests allow us to assess a candidate's practical skills in a real-world context. This approach helps us gauge their problem-solving abilities and hands-on expertise.

2. AI-Enhanced Screening:

We leverage AI tools to streamline the initial screening process, ensuring we spend time interviewing only the most promising candidates.

3. Behavioral Assessments:

Utilizing tools like DISC assessments, we gain insights into a candidate's behavioral traits and work styles. This helps us understand how they would fit into our team dynamics and contribute to our company culture.

4. Continuous Learning and Development:

Once onboard, employees are enrolled in continuous learning programs powered by AI and machine learning. This ensures they are always up-to-date with the latest industry practices and technological advancements.

5. Employee Development Systems (EDS):

We use EDS for ongoing employee development, ensuring each team member is consistently growing and evolving in their role.

By integrating modern technological solutions and innovative strategies into our employee management and recruitment processes, we're not just competing on service; we're setting new benchmarks for excellence in the industry. Our approach is designed to attract, develop, and retain the best talent, ensuring that our team is equipped to provide unparalleled service to our clients.

Spark of Awesome, Not on Price Technique:

Use technology to standardize processes.

In an era where technology is king, our business underwent a transformative change by systemically integrating eight different kinds of AI. Within a single week, we created over 1100 detailed policies and procedures, resulting in a robust seven-hour onboarding process for our employees. This systemic and technological overhaul has not only streamlined our operations but significantly boosted our revenue by 30%. We attribute this remarkable growth to our cutting-edge onboarding and training techniques, including the use of VR glasses and other advanced technologies.

The easiest way to build systems in your business, is to have all of the key players to sit around a room with flipchart paper and sticky notes. Everyone gets a different color based on their functional area. That is the beginning of a process.

Are you ready to dive in deeper?

Let's take some time to dive into the questions we asked earlier in the chapter.

What can you put into place that would allow you to hire smarter?

Who needs to be at the table?

Are you prepared to take this on? It is transformative, but it is a huge commitment!

CHAPTER 10

Pulling it All Together

Chapter: Mastering the Art of Excellence: A Guide to Competing on Awesome In the dynamic business world, thriving on excellence rather than just competing on price is the key to sustainable success. Embracing this philosophy, we've developed a comprehensive approach that amalgamates innovative technology, exceptional service, and top-tier talent. Here's an expanded overview of how we've implemented these principles to create a standout business model.

1. Harnessing Technology for Superior Service:

Automated Systems: Implement cutting-edge technology to automate and streamline processes. This includes customer relationship management systems, automated scheduling, and digital invoicing to enhance efficiency and accuracy.

Digital Training Tools: Utilize virtual reality and AI-based training modules to upskill employees, ensuring they deliver consistent, high-quality service.

2. Targeting Underserved Markets with Excellence:

Identifying Gaps: Conduct market research to identify underserved areas or niche markets. By focusing on these areas, you can tailor your services to meet specific needs that competitors may overlook.

Customized Solutions: Develop bespoke solutions that cater specifically to these markets, ensuring your services are unique, highly relevant, and valuable to your target audience.

3. Recruiting and Nurturing Top Talent:

Selective Hiring: Employ a rigorous hiring process beyond traditional criteria. Look for candidates with the necessary skills that align with your company's values and vision.

Ongoing Development: Invest in continuous training and development programs. Encourage a culture of learning and growth, which benefits your employees and enhances the overall quality of your services.

4. Innovation as a Core Principle:

Encourage Creativity: Foster an environment where innovation is encouraged. Regular brainstorming sessions and open forums for ideas can lead to breakthroughs in how services are delivered.

Adapting to Change: Stay abreast of industry trends and be willing to pivot or adapt your strategies to stay ahead of the curve.

5. Rigorous Tracking and Adaptation:

Data-Driven Decisions: Implement systems to track key performance indicators (KPIs) and customer feedback. Use this data to make informed decisions and continuous improvements.

Regular Reviews: Conduct periodic assessments of processes and strategies to identify areas for improvement and ensure alignment with business goals.

6. Documenting and Sharing Success:

Brand Storytelling: Document your journey and share your success stories. This enhances your brand image and is a testament to your commitment to excellence.

Engaging Content: Create engaging content that showcases your services, customer testimonials, and the impact of your work. Utilize social media and digital platforms to widen your reach.

7. Maximizing and Managing Reviews:

Active Engagement: Encourage customers to leave reviews and actively engage with the feedback received. This improves online visibility and demonstrates your commitment to customer satisfaction.

Reputation Management: Regularly monitor and manage your online reputation. Address negative reviews constructively and leverage positive reviews to build trust and credibility.

8. Awards and Recognition:

Strategic Applications: Identify and apply for awards that align with your business values and services. Winning these awards can significantly enhance your brand's reputation and visibility.

Celebrating Achievements: Share your achievements with your team and customers. Celebrating these milestones fosters a sense of pride and reinforces your commitment to excellence.

9. Thought Leadership:

Expert Insights: Position yourself as a thought leader in your industry by sharing insights, trends, and expert opinions. This can be through blogs, podcasts, webinars, or speaking engagements.

Community Involvement: Participate in industry forums, discussions, and events to stay connected and contribute to the broader community.

10. Community Involvement and Social Responsibility:

Giving Back: Integrate community service into your business model. Engage in philanthropic activities, and support causes that resonate with your brand and team.

Sustainable Practices: Adopt eco-friendly and sustainable practices in your operations. This benefits the environment and appeals to a growing segment of environmentally conscious consumers.

It has not been easy......

In the spirit of raw authenticity, I must confess that the path of our business has been far from a seamless journey. There's a common thread that binds all entrepreneurs, and it's woven with the challenges and the grit it takes to overcome them. Our story is no exception. The year 2019 was a tumultuous chapter for us; we teetered on the brink of losing everything we had built. This period was marked by a series of missteps— misjudged hires I made, lapses in oversight due to my extensive travels, and a lack of robust systems and key performance indicators (KPIs) to guide us. The culmination of these oversights was a toxic culture, a crisis for which I shoulder the blame. Leadership starts at the top, and I faltered.

Yet, the journey through this storm has led to a renaissance of our company's spirit. Now, when the sound of laughter and the evidence of our team's camaraderie and mutual support echo through the office, my heart is lifted. The transformation wasn't easy; the road was fraught with personal and professional trials that tested the limits of our resilience. The strain it placed on my relationship with my spouse, the emotional toll it took on me, and the financial strain that required me to juggle three jobs just to keep us afloat, was nearly insurmountable. It's a testament to the life of an entrepreneur: a life chosen not for its ease, but for its intensity and the passion that fuels us. It's a calling that demands daily affirmations of purpose and resolve. It's a relentless pursuit of a vision that demands every ounce of our being, even when the hurdles seem insurmountable. This is the unvarnished truth of our journey, a testament to the fact that even when the path is rocky, our unwavering commitment and passion are the very essence of our entrepreneurial spirit.

And Finally, the Elephants:

In the heart of Africa, under the vast and endless sky, there's a profound lesson unfolding on the savannah: strength, community, and resilience. It's the story of the elephant circle, a powerful display of unity and protection among these majestic creatures. As entrepreneurs and individuals navigating the complexities of life, especially those of us with unique challenges like ADHD, there's much to learn from this natural wonder.

Imagine a serene African landscape where herds of elephants roam freely, their gentle might echo across the plains. Among them is a mother elephant, a symbol of nurturing and wisdom. When danger looms or when she's at her most vulnerable, an extraordinary thing happens. The herd forms an impenetrable circle around her, with the most robust and most able elephants on the outside and the more vulnerable in the middle, safeguarding the mother and her calf.

This elephant circle is a metaphor for the community we must build and cherish in our own lives. Sometimes, you are the mother elephant, weary in need of support and protection. You carry the weight of your dreams and struggles, much like the mother elephant carries the future of her herd. In these moments, it's crucial to have a circle of strength around you – your tribe of fellow entrepreneurs, those who share the unique journey of ADHD, and those who understand the resilience required to overcome personal battles.

There will also be times when you are the elephant on the outside, strong, vigilant, and capable. In these moments, you can offer protection and support to others in your community who are in need. Your strength and experience become the shield and comfort for someone else who is during their own struggle.

The beauty of the elephant circle lies in its fluidity – roles change, today's protectors might be tomorrow's protected, and this ebb and flow continues. It's a beautiful dance of mutual support, empathy, and understanding. In this dance, it's essential to find and nurture your community. Surround yourself with individuals who understand your journey and complement your strengths and weaknesses. In the company of fellow entrepreneurs, you find wisdom and experience. Among your ADHD brothers and sisters, you find empathy and unique perspectives. This community becomes your fortress against the world's challenges, just as the circle of elephants becomes an unbreakable shield against the dangers of the wild.

So, seek out your tribe, nurture these relationships, and be ready to play your part, whether in the circle's center or on its protective perimeter. Remember, in unity, there's strength, and in understanding, there's power. Your community, your elephant circle, is not just about protection; it's about growing together, learning from each other, and moving forward with a shared sense of purpose and resilience.

Together, as a united front, you can face the wilds of entrepreneurship and life's unpredictable challenges, just as the majestic elephants of the African savannah do – with dignity, strength, and an unyielding bond.

About The Author

Susan Frew is not just an author; she's a testament to the transformative power of embracing one's unique traits as strengths. Her journey from the corporate realms of technology and AT&T Wireless to the entrepreneurial challenges of the plumbing and heating industry encapsulates a tale of resilience, innovation, and relentless drive.

In the corporate sphere, Susan honed her prowess in business development and strategic planning. Her transition to entrepreneurship with Sunshine Plumbing Heating Air in Denver, Colorado, marks a story of grit and strategic ingenuity. Under her leadership as co-owner and President, she metamorphosed a modest venture into a multi-million-dollar success story.

Beyond her industry-specific achievements, Susan's influence stretches across various sectors.

Susan's journey is punctuated by personal battles with health challenges, including multiple injuries and a rare disease. Rather than seeing these as setbacks, Susan embraces her

ADHD, OCD, and the aftermath of head injuries as her unique business superpowers. These attributes have sharpened her focus, fueled her creativity, and endowed her with a unique perspective on problem-solving and business strategy.

A charismatic speaker, Susan has captivated audiences at TEDx and other prestigious platforms, sharing her insights on resilience and the transformative power of adversity. Her book is more than a business manual; it's a window into her soul, revealing her belief in making a meaningful difference alongside achieving business success.

Passionate about empowering women in the trades and advocating for innovative business approaches, Susan's commitment extends beyond her company. Her community work and her efforts to inspire through her writing and speaking engagements reflect a philosophy where success is intertwined with making a positive impact.

Away from her professional endeavors, Susan cherishes moments with her husband, William, her family, and her love for travel. Her story is a beacon of hope and an example of how embracing one's unique qualities can lead to unprecedented success. P.S. Chat Gpt wrote this bio!

www.ingramcontent.com/pod-product-compliance
Lightning Source LLC
Chambersburg PA
CBHW032029290526
45786CB00011B/1177